ABOUT THE AUTHOR

Born in 1994 and raised in Connecticut, Michael Slaughter is a recent graduate of Sacred Heart University (class of 2016) with a double major in accounting and finance. Graduating with a cumulative 3.96 GPA, he received numerous scholarships and prestigious accolades from both his University and nationally. He was a starting player on the Division 1 Men's Lacrosse Team and had numerous other involvements on campus.

In his junior year of college, Michael published his first book entitled "From Failure to Triumph: Inspiring Stories to Help You Overcome Challenges and Achieve Success" in the motivational/inspirational category. Holding numerous book signings and available in both print and e-book, he has heard welcoming feedback from all it has inspired and his book reached the #1 best-selling spot in his category for the Amazon Kindle.

Michael founded his own online collectible card business at 10 years old and proceeded to grow it to become one of the top sellers in the world in his industry. With a prominent online brand and an average annual growth rate of 82% over the 12 years he ran it, Michael sold his business after he graduated from college to pursue a career in the financial markets. The experiences and knowledge he acquired over these 12 years were invaluable and developed within him, due to the vast similarities, his strong passion for the markets.

He currently works in the investment management industry looking to establish a prominent career. Michael resides in New York City, and in his free time, he enjoys exercising, surfing, fishing, and reading.

How to Start a Successful Online Business

How to Start a Successful Online Business

A Framework from Experience

Michael L. Slaughter

How to Start a Successful Online Business

mslaughter.business@gmail.com

Printed in the United States of America

ISBN: 978-0-9966049-2-5

I would like to thank my mother, Linda, for all her invaluable help and unconditional love. I have learned so much from her and am forever grateful.

Table of Contents

1.	**From Scratch**	11
2.	**The Benefits of an Online Business**	15
3.	**Find Your Passion**	19
4.	**Identify Your Niche**	23
5.	**The Value of Your Brand**	27
6.	**Acquiring and Selling Products**	31
7.	**The Importance of Customer Service**	37
8.	**The Power in Numbers**	43
9.	**Creating a Marketing Plan**	47
10.	**Hiring Employees**	53
11.	**The Entrepreneurial Mindset**	57
12.	**Conclusion**	61

1

From Scratch

While many entrepreneurs try to bait you into paying an outlandish amount of money to learn how to start an online business, I do not believe in that. When there is already risk in pursuing your online business idea, why increase it even more by paying someone who may not be rightfully qualified thousands of dollars? This is my motive in wanting to provide you a framework for online business success backed by my personal experience through a quick and affordable book. Entrepreneurs are the backbone to our global economy, and the world deserves to be blessed with that idea you so badly want to make a reality. In the following chapters, I provide tips from my personal experience to help you build the necessary framework of knowledge needed to replicate my online business success and travel this entrepreneurial journey with confidence.

Before I describe the framework, it is helpful for you to hear my story so you can understand the process and amount of time I spent building my online business. As a child, I was very entrepreneurial but left with the dilemma that all children face, which was being too young to work. I decided I would make money in any possible way no matter how much I had to learn or how unorthodox for my age.

At 10 years old in 2004, I decided to sell my small Pokémon card collection on eBay along with other used belongings that had been sitting under my bed to earn a little money. Upon selling my old Pokémon collection for $10, I realized a strong niche existed online for collectible cards due to the inefficient, traditional card collecting process of purchasing card packs in retail stores. With my personal collection sold, I needed to acquire more cards; thus, I began reaching out to friends and classmates in my middle school to sell their old collections they no longer wanted and agreed to split the profits with them. After selling a lot of my friends' cards and seeing continued success, I needed to acquire more inventory and began to post flyers in grocery stores around my local area. It stated on the flyers I would pay cash for collectible card collections, and kids were thrilled they could sell their old collection and receive money to purchase a new video game. I did very well acquiring inventory through this method; however, I eventually went through a large portion of these local resources and had to consider other unique ways to accumulate inventory to fulfill the strong online demand. As a result, I expanded my horizons and began to purchase card collections across the country on eBay (which was the main platform I was selling on at the time) by filtering daily through close to 100,000 different listings in the marketplace.

In my first year of selling, I had sales of about $500 – which was a decent amount for a 10 year old. As I continued to acquire more inventory and learn further about the vast intricacies of running a business, I became much more efficient in my processes each year. I began to appreciate the value of hard work and time management, and I worked to better understand my industry. Three years later at the age of 13, I created my own eBay store and expanded my sales reach beyond the United States to international markets.

As my sales continued to grow, I understood to a greater extent and became more attentive to the importance of customer service and brand reputation, which allowed me to position myself towards the high-end of the market. By positioning myself in this area, it provided me the ability to charge premium prices over my competitors and achieve average gross margins of 76%.

In my college years, I expanded to the Amazon marketplace and also revamped my entire inventory system, photo catalog, product descriptions, cost management processes, and shipping procedures. In addition, I shifted focus from predominantly selling a variety of Pokémon merchandise to focusing on a niche with it (complete card sets) that had very strong demand due to the price savings and convenience obtained by the customer when purchasing an entire Pokémon card set. This niche had not been fully developed yet, and continuing to build on my successes and brand recognition, I soon became the #1 seller in this area of the market along with being one of the overall top Pokémon sellers in the world.

As a sophomore in college, I undertook the initiative to expand beyond eBay and Amazon by building my own e-commerce website to further strengthen my brand, increase margins, and offer a larger product catalog. After six months of very intensive work, I launched my website with close to 10,000 unique products and saw great success over the coming few years.

In 2015, my last full calendar year of selling – which was also the busiest time of my college career – I achieved sales of about $200,000 and an average annual growth rate of over 80% since inception. With a strong brand reputation, high sales growth, and worldwide customer base, I undertook the process in my senior year to sell my business. Teaching myself a great deal about private enterprise valuations, pitch books, and the due diligence process, I ended up selling my online business in June 2016 at the age of 22 to two buyers – wow what a feeling!

Keeping my background story above a bit brief, I wanted to explain the broad development of my online business to give you an idea of how much had to be learned through personal experience over my 12 years of work – and you now have access to this special information. All it takes is for someone to be equipped with the knowledge needed to create a successful online business – coupled with the passion, work ethic, and commitment – to be able to start their own thriving venture.

2

The Benefits of an Online Business

We live in the most abundant time in the history of the world, but so many people fail to see this. There has never been a more exciting era with such abundant opportunities. Each day new millionaires are made, new products are invented, and new businesses blossom. We all have technology available to us that allows anyone to start an online business with ease; all it takes is the understanding and perseverance to join that special group of people that followed their dream and started their own successful online business.

Even if you already have a day job, you can still start an online business by working on it in your free time at night and/or on the weekends. Understand the majority of online businesses are started part-time in someone's free hours until the business grows large enough to require full-time attention. Instead of watching T.V. or browsing the internet, utilize your time in a more meaningful way. You can accomplish so much if you chose to stay disciplined and be productive with your countless hours of free time.

The benefits of starting an online business are endless – to start off, anyone has the ability! You do not need a large amount of money or even a warehouse; you can simply start it from the comfort of your own home. As previously mentioned, I started my online business from my childhood home with a $10 Pokémon card collection; even if you are in financial distress or do not have a college degree, you can still get started like I did. Since you are working out of your own home (initially), you not only have the comfort of not having to travel somewhere, but you also have much lower overhead expenses since you do not have any additional property costs. Eventually, you may decide to expand to a warehouse, but your online business will be much larger at that point.

Another great benefit of starting your own online business is being your own boss. You are in charge of your own destiny and do not have to report to anyone. No one will tell you when or what to do – that responsibility is all on you. You determine when and for how long you work. If you are a morning person and prefer to work very early, or if you are a night owl and like to work at midnight, that choice is completely up to you. You set your schedule and determine when things will get done.

Due to the ever-improving technology around us, I had opportunities to work on my online business while waiting for a dentist appointment, sitting on a train, walking in between classes in college, and in other daily life situations.

You can utilize all this free time that people often do not use productively to work on your business and increase your income. All of this extra time spent working throughout the day adds up and you will be surprised at how much more can be accomplished.

Lastly, and one of my favorite aspects of having an online business, is the ability to earn money while doing life's other meaningful activities. Online businesses are a hybrid source of income mixed between passive and active. For example, you will put in time shipping orders and communicating with customers, but you will also earn sales all throughout the day even when not working. The greatest source of income is one that does not directly trade your time for money – and that is the powerful benefit of an online business. Once the inventory is for sale, anyone has the ability to purchase it regardless of where or what you are doing at that moment.

You now understand some of the desirable benefits of running your own online business, but you need to be equipped with the right knowledge to ensure you achieve success in starting yours, and that begins with identifying your passion.

3

Find Your Passion

One of the most critical aspects that determines the success of your online business is whether you are actually passionate about the products you sell. Without passion, you will lack the foresight to see emerging trends in the marketplace, the ability to excite your customers, and most importantly, you will not want to put the necessary work in to be successful.

In order to be the best at any endeavor (not just in business but applicable to life), you have to be passionate. For example, individuals who truly enjoy designing clothing will work in ways to understand their market better and grow to become the most knowledgeable in their field – and easily surpass their competition in the process. They will want to wake up early and go to bed to late, and everything in between will contain thoughts on how to design their clothing in more unique ways. The more knowledge you acquire about the particular industry you sell in, the more creative you will be and the quicker you will expand.

In order to best assess your interests, go grab a piece of paper and pen – this is your idea sheet you will now work on. Take a few minutes to write down any particular industries that excite you such as drones, shoes, cameras, jewelry, etc. Then, evaluate your current knowledge about each industry you wrote down, and if it is lacking in depth, broadly research more about it to identify its trends. Even if you know a handful about the industry already, it is likely only surface knowledge and you will soon discover how much more there is to learn. Some industries have larger markets and are more lucrative than others; however, it is most important to find what you feel strongly about and want to pursue further. This process takes time so do not rush it.

After performing research and evaluating your findings, you should narrow down your list to one or two particular industries of interest. As a side note, many of the greatest companies created a new market for a product that consumers did not know they wanted until it was introduced. While this is possible for you, it will be an easier challenge to sell in an online market that is already established with strong demand and that is what this book focuses on.

Once you have narrowed down your list, you need to decide between your final two industries of interest, so spend time to intensely research each market further. Your previous research when finalizing your list probably consisted of further surface research that lacked depth and detail, and that is the purpose behind the research in this stage. Through a variety of online marketplaces, analyze the best-selling items within each industry, the demographics of the customers, if the demand is cyclical, the degree of change each industry is experiencing, and other important information needed to better understand each industry's dynamics. Analyze the various competitors that exist in each market and whether it is saturated by a handful of big or small sellers. If it is saturated by the latter, economies of scale may help you achieve lower prices than the other small sellers, while with the former, it is likely the big sellers struggle with quality customer service or product differentiation, and this presents an opportunity to steal market share despite the likelihood of having a higher cost structure.

Very importantly, consider the overall size of the market and growth opportunities that exist – some of which may not be currently visible if the industry is new or changing. You do not want to put all your efforts into an industry that is in the process of dying or in one that is so small there is not enough room for you to grow to an adequate size. For example, if one of the industries of interest on your idea sheet was MP3 players – a little research would show you that the MP3 market has died off to more advanced forms of music players and that this is an area of the music industry you would want to stay away from. On the other hand, if you wrote down the collectible stamp market, you would find that this is a thriving industry with a very long history of being a popular hobby, and thus, it is currently both a large market and one that has room for continued growth.

Finding the right industry to start an online business in is a time-intensive process that requires a lot of patience and creative thought. If you jump too quickly in the wrong industry, you will unnecessarily waste your time and money and come to the realization that some patient research could have provided you with most of the answers about why that specific market was not ideal to enter. Once you have done your proper due diligence and have selected an industry, it is time to identify your niche.

4

Identify Your Niche

Not just in business, but in life in general, the more specialized you are in terms of your work, the greater the value you will be able to add in your particular endeavor. One of the best ways to build a brand and strong online presence is by focusing on a niche within a specific industry and becoming known for that area of specialty. When you think of a specific product – let's say a cellphone – which company instantly comes to mind? It is most likely Apple, and that is due to their intense focus on dominating that market. While Apple is very specialized in selling the iPhone, they do still sell a variety of other products; however, they concentrated a large amount of their efforts on a specific niche and succeeded in their quest.

Finding a niche often requires you to become very familiar with a unique marketplace so you can understand patterns and trends that are not easily identifiable, and you will most likely need to start selling first in order to gain that knowledge. Your niche may not be the item you sell the most of, but rather a lucrative opportunity that you see exists and wish to capitalize on. With my own online business, I specialized in complete card sets, which were very time efficient to sell and contributed to most of my annual revenue; however, they accounted for less than 20% of my total sales volume.

As you begin to sell online, look for niches in your market that are either underdeveloped or (if applicable) that consist of standardized products. If an area of the market consists only of standardized products, product differentiation can help you gain market share, and it is achieved by selling a unique good that a buyer can only purchase from you and not a competing seller. Your customer base will be more permanent – unless the product becomes obsolete or a product of better value enters the marketplace – when you sell a unique good as no other seller will have an exact replica of your product.

On the other hand, an online business can specialize in a niche selling standardized products with economies of scale. This means the business aims to be the lowest cost producer, which in turn allows it to have the lowest price in the market. In a sense, there is nothing proprietary about this business model besides its low cost structure. If another business comes along and achieves a greater economies of scale, the original business will no longer be the lowest cost provider and will lose significant market share over time. Both types of online businesses have their pros and cons;

however, product differentiation is the most unique and difficult for a competitor to replicate.

After you identify your niche, it is imperative you start becoming the most knowledgeable in that area. By doing so, you will be able to adapt to the dynamic and changing marketplace, discover new opportunities, and fulfill the desires of consumers in creative ways. As you provide superior products and quality service, your brand reputation will strengthen.

5

The Value of Your Brand

The value of any business is determined by its brand. Most corporate acquisitions attribute a significant portion of the purchase premium to the goodwill of a business (i.e. the brand and intangible value) because that is the most pertinent determining factor in its continued success. If you ever wish to sell the online business you commence, the offer price will be largely based upon its position in the industry and its brand value. For example, all else being equal, would you rather acquire Disney or a media provider unbeknown to the public? Quite obviously, almost everyone would prefer Disney because of its positioning in the industry and what it means in the eyes of consumers when they hear the word.

The success of your online business relies upon the maintenance of your brand image. There is no quicker way to lose your faithful customers, like numerous large companies have done over the years, than by alienating them. This is often the end result when a business drastically changes its business model in attempt to identify with an entirely different level of the market. If your online business identifies with the low-end of the market, and you suddenly switch your products to focus on the high-end, consumers in the high-end will not identify with your brand, and you will have alienated your customers in the low-end – quite the hopeless outcome.

To start off, ask yourself what attributes you want a consumer to associate your online business with when they hear its name or see its logo? Is it – exceptional customer service, luxury products, affordability, fast shipping, or another combination of attributes? Spend time dwelling on this subject, and when you have decided on the specific attributes, write it down on your idea sheet. Writing it down increases accountability and ensures you do not deviate in the future from what is important to you.

Your business logo and slogan should be identifiable and relatable to the industry you sell in. A consumer, unaware of your business or industry, should have an understanding of the products you sell just by looking at your logo. When designing it, I always prefer something bold, bright, or unique – something that would visibly stand out if compared to a handful of other logos in your industry. In regards to your slogan, while a sentence that rhymes can seem cheesy, it is very effective. People have an ability to remember song lyrics and sentences that rhyme better than a simple sentence, so incorporating a brief, clever sentence that rhymes as your slogan will be memorable.

In addition, always focus on the high-end of the market when possible. Premium products, while usually superior in quality compared to low-end products, mainly derive their price from the value consumers attach to the brand. In the online marketplace especially, counterfeit products or dishonest sellers can be somewhat frequent, and it is that strong brand reputation that can allow you to achieve higher margins by charging a premium price for a somewhat identical product over another smaller, less-known seller. While you can excel being a low-cost provider, it is a far more difficult area to compete in – the reason being the most valuable aspect of your brand is your low price. As well, other competitors may try to undercut your price for such an extended period of time that they force you out of business; similar to what temporary monopolies have attempted in the past. Most businesses can easily compete on price with a large capital base, but it is a far greater challenge to compete against a strong brand known for its unique and quality products.

Your brand is maintained through effort – it takes dedication to provide customers with quality products and superior service on every transaction. Never become shortsighted and sacrifice short-term profits for long-term value. Along the way, your greed may make you ponder the temporarily lucrative situation of selling slightly lower quality or providing less customer service to enhance profit, but this destroys more long-term value than you could ever reap in this short period. Focus on creating brand viability and positioning your online business in the marketplace exactly where you want it to be, and the fruit of your labor will be long-lasting.

6

Acquiring and Selling Products

Relevant to all types of online businesses, it is imperative you always purchase your products or raw materials in bulk quantity. Similar to shopping at Costco where you would expect discounts for purchasing large amounts of consumer goods, it is the same when acquiring business supplies or products – it will always be cheaper to purchase in bulk than in small volume. For example, an online business that ships packages should purchase tape, envelopes, and other packaging supplies in large quantity to lower the cost of these standardized and essential items. When I switched from purchasing tape individually to bulk orders, I lowered my unit cost by around 70%. Regardless of your business model, the materials or products you use/sell should be purchased in large quantity – to an extent. It is important, especially in the initial testing phase of your online business, that you do not order a massive amount of an item before you know if you can even sell it. Anytime you over anticipate demand and purchase too much quantity, it not only increases your opportunity cost (as the funds could have been used to buy and sell other inventory or have even been invested), but the only way to dispose of it is by liquidating at low prices for a loss. Be cognizant of supply and demand, and only when you know demand is strong is it then safe to proceed in ordering those materials/products in larger quantity.

One of the biggest questions people ask is… how does one acquire inventory? With my online business, I always carried close to 100,000 cards in stock at any given time, and I used a handful of different inventory acquisition methods over the years. Examples of great places to purchase goods for your online business include eBay, Amazon, Craigslist, garage sales, estate sales, or even posting flyers around the city or town you live in specifying the items you want to buy like I did when I was starting out. Out of the above venues, I found eBay to have the most abundant opportunities for inventory. It is ironic that you can buy a product in quantity on eBay and then proceed to sell it in that same marketplace with high margins, but this only occurs if you possess the proper knowledge. When you are specialized in an industry, you will understand what specific online searches reveal the best opportunities to obtain inventory at a low cost.

As a general concept, a product that is sold in bulk with other related or non-related products will sell for a lower cost per unit than that single product in bulk by itself. Businesses (and people) do not like purchasing unnecessary items alongside something they want, so these multi-bulk deals can end up being the most profitable. The reason people sell bulk in this manner online is due to the convenience and ease in unloading everything at once rather than selling each item individually. As a personal example, I was searching through eBay and once found someone selling Pokémon cards and Pokémon marbles together on auction at a current bid price of $80; however, I had only sold cards at this point and had no experience or knowledge with Pokémon marbles. I quickly identified the value in the cards, which was around $350, but the marbles remained a mystery. I researched the market for Pokémon marbles, and swiftly discovered that the marbles possessed value and more than I had anticipated too. The marbles ended up being worth around $300, so the total value of this $80 lot was over $650. If all these items were listed individually or even if the cards and marbles were separated into different respective lots, the seller would have received far more than $80 for over $650 worth of merchandise. From this purchase and the research that coincided with it, I identified that the Pokémon marble market had high margins with limited competition, and then going forward, I began to search for and acquire more of them. This example of purchasing semi-related products in bulk is one of the numerous ways your online business can acquire low-cost inventory and at the same time unexpectedly expand into a different niche within your industry.

Along with the service you provide each customer, your

products are the main ingredients in determining your online business success. Whether you make custom items or resell products, the goods customers purchase from you define to a large extent their happiness in each respective transaction. To place an estimate on a rather subjective data point, I would say 75% of customer happiness comes from the product while the other 25% comes from the service/logistics of the transaction.

If you are selling in the high-end market (which is the ideal location for margins and brand value), it is critical that each unit you sell be of the same quality. Unreliable, defective, or broken products can destroy the trust consumers' have in your products. Think of all the situations where companies have had to recall a product due to a safety concern or defective component, and the simultaneous backlash and negative publicity the company had to fight as a result. When this type of incident arises, consumers take their money elsewhere and it can then be difficult to regain trust and loyalty. If you ever experience an unfortunate situation similar to this, damage control is essential to ensure you thwart the fire of negative propaganda that will arise around your products and online business.

Depending on your industry (especially technology), testing your product repetitively for any issues is critical to your success. While this is not applicable to certain items, you still need to ensure all your products are of the same quality. For example, if you are selling clothing, the fabric must be made of the same grade and the clothing should not have any lose strings or stitching mistakes. If the quality of the clothing varies in each of your transactions, the result will be dissatisfied customers that feel your products are inferior and do not justify their price. Consumers want what they pay for, and if they do not get it, their voice will be heard by you or the public. If you are reselling previously owned goods, you need to ensure they are 100% authentic and/or the product works to its full extent. Businesses have been forced to shut down in the past for selling unbeknown counterfeit or defective products.

Depending on the online marketplace, every product you sell needs to include a high-resolution photo and precise description that provides information about the product. Buyers can be skeptical purchasing from an online business, especially one without years of experience, and nothing scares away a potential customer more than a blurry photo with a vague description of the item available for sale. You want to be as clear as possible so the potential customer is not confused in the slightest with what is being offered.

Lastly, applicable to any type of product you sell, there must be something different about your product when compared to your competitors. Regardless of price, which we know being the low-cost seller is a very difficult business model to sustain, your product needs to be unlike other products in the marketplace – i.e. better capabilities, more features, higher quality, top service that comes along with it, etc. In my situation, even though I was a re-seller, I differentiated myself by providing 100% authentic, quality products with exceptional customer service and fast shipping. When a consumer is presented with two identically priced products from two different businesses, your product should be the one he/she wants to grab because of your differentiating aspects – the only way to maintain, increase, or steal market share is by mastering this.

To stay on top of any emerging trends in your industry, study your competition like you do your own business model. If you notice a competitor shifting its sales or product strategy, carefully monitor the success of the competitor's new approach, and then either implement it yourself (if it is successful) or improve upon the idea. By closely monitoring your competition, you will limit the potential for market share loss to occur.

Once you sell a product, the service you provide after payment has been received for the transaction is the remaining 25% that will determine the happiness of each customer.

7

The Importance of Customer Service

The way a transaction is handled makes a lasting impression on the customer because many online businesses do not want to go the extra mile. Very large businesses often struggle with customer support and diligent communication when they sell to individual consumers due to their volume of daily sales, but these post-transaction services are invaluable in the sales process and are a differentiating way to add value.

Once consumers purchase your product, they want to feel that your interests still align with theirs after the sale. Some businesses change their behavior after receiving payment and customers quickly notice it. When a business acts in this manor, customers are left with a distasteful experience even if the product they receive matched their expectations. Individuals that have negative experiences with your online business will be quick to notify their friends (who share similar interests) or even others online that your business is not reputable. Online businesses known for this type of poor reputation have a very low rate of repeat customers, and eventually, a low growth rate in new customers as all the small damage adds up. It is vital you convert as many unique buyers into repeat customers to ensure long-term success. Post-transaction services are how a reputation and brand are built - and positive word of mouth from your past customers is the most potent form of marketing.

Consumers have to place more trust in an online business than a brick and mortar store because they cannot physically see the goods they are purchasing online, which leaves room for online businesses to more easily engage in suspicious activity. With countless online businesses over the years traveling down this unfortunate path, it has left distrust with consumers. Buyers are more careful and spend extra time screening a business before making a purchase, but as a result, they tend to be more loyal once they find a reputable seller. If you tend to purchase a specific type of good online, it is far easier to go directly to the online business you trust than it is to look up the good in numerous marketplaces from a variety of different sellers for the absolute lowest price. This is why providing great service to your customers helps build long-term relationships as they will frequently purchase from you again in the future when they have further needs.

For every transaction, you should notify your customers once you have received their payment to ensure they know their order went through successfully; afterwards, you will package their items for shipment. The presentation and protection of the merchandise is an essential and often overlooked aspect by businesses, so ensure you take the utmost care in packaging and protecting the items. This helps prevent the possibility of any damage occurring during transit along with the merchandise looking neat and organized upon arrival. For the complete Pokémon card sets I sold, which were usually around $200-300 per set, I always took extra care in protecting the collectible cards by placing them in card sleeves, which were then placed in a folder with bubble wrap added around it, and then put in a thick bubble envelope with "fragile" stickers on the outside of the package. If a customer purchased an expensive card set and I had shipped it with no form of protection and in a worn envelope (granted it does not get damaged), he/she would have instantly felt a lack of respect from me as a seller and not purchase again. Packaging the item in a careful and organized way shows customers that you not only respect the item they purchased, but that you also focus on the "little things" in every transaction.

Besides exceptional customer service, all else held equal, consumers will purchase from another online business if they know the item arrives to them in a much quicker manner. So much work is put into all the other areas of your business that you do not want to let a delay in shipping be the demerit that weakens your sales performance. For all your orders, try to ship out the purchased items within 24 hours of payment. This can be difficult, especially considering all the other responsibilities you may have, but online consumers have accepted fast shipping as a universal standard due to the effectiveness of Amazon and myriad of other large companies. While a business has no ability to control the speed at which a package is delivered once it is in the hands of the post office, most packages arrive within their stated delivery window assuming you shipped the order on time. Always purchase a tracking number for every package as the minimal increase in cost is your best insurance against the occasional fraudulent buyer; however, heavy packages will automatically come with a tracking number due to the shipping method required.

Once you ship the items out, send the customers a shipment notification letting them know they should receive their merchandise shortly. Provide them with the tracking number and reassure them that you would be glad to assist them with any questions or concerns they may have. If customers are dissatisfied with the items they receive, professionally work with them over the issue(s) they have – do not become angry or defensive. There may be situations where you need to be firm with your customers because of an issue unrelated to your merchandise or service (like they want their own custom return policy other than what you specified); in this situation, it is acceptable to be less lenient but still professional in your communication. You will come across customers that only find the negative no matter how much effort you put in to help them, so understand you cannot please everyone. Use these problematic buyers as learning lessons on how you can better assist your future customers, and once again, do not argue or yell at them. If you do, this will cause a handful of them to seek revenge and try to damage your business' reputation.

Your return policy should be clearly stated on all your products, but also remind your customers of your policy by sending them a copy inside their package. It will help avoid any confusion and assure that they are aware of your refund procedures in the event they wish to return their items. If an issue arises, always offer your customers a store credit if possible instead of a refund; if they receive a refund, it is highly likely that they will take their business elsewhere. A store credit not only maintains the payment from the concerning transactions, but it can strengthen your relationship with your customers as they will look to purchase other items you are offering with their credit. With the assumption you handle all aspects of this new transaction professionally, the previous unfortunate event that resulted in a customer receiving a store credit gave you the opportunity to leave him/her with a completely different and positive experience.

Selling a quality product alongside fast shipping and meaningful service will result in happy customers time after time. Focus on adding the most value to the marketplace, and you will eliminate the problematic customers to the best a business can.

8

The Power in Numbers

Referred to as "the language of business," accounting is one of the most critical areas of business you must understand. No online business can successfully operate without tight financial controls in place that monitor the daily cash inflows and outflows. Without an accounting system, you will not be able to assess the profitability of your online business, manage your expenses, or assess all the other important financial aspects.

There are numerous platforms you can use to keep track of your accounting records and the most easily available is Microsoft Excel. You should have an income statement (that keeps track of your revenues, expenses, and profit), a balance sheet (that keeps track of your assets, liabilities, and equity), and a cash flow statement (that tracks the cash coming in and out of your business). These statements are vital to understanding how well your online business is doing financially. When recording your revenues and expenses, include (to an extent) the most detail you can. This will give you the ability to perform a thorough analysis on your business' logistics and operations when looking back on past transactions. For example, when I had previously studied my accounting records, I came to the conclusion that selling individual cards for $1 through eBay resulted in near zero profitability despite having solid customer demand. As a result, I stopped selling these low-priced individual cards on eBay and opened my own website. I was able to match this strong demand through my website while removing the extra costs associated with eBay, and I implemented a small minimum order size as well. This turned near 0% margins into around 80-90% margins. If I did not have this information available from my extensive record keeping, my online business would not have been operating efficiently and I would have missed out on a critical opportunity.

Your accounting statements should be updated at least daily, or if you have heavy sales volume, more frequently throughout the day. As well, you will want to keep track of customer addresses, emails, and any other information that may be useful for you in terms of marketing or business assessment. If you keep track of emails, you will have an email list of past customers that you could reach out to with special promotions. By keeping track of customers' addresses, you will be able to do geographical analysis to see where most of your customers are located, which may help you with marketing or in adjusting your business strategy to specific regions of the world.

The more detail you record for each transaction, the more useful your accounting records will be to you and any others down the road who you may interact with such as consultants or new business partners. Especially if you ever need outside capital or wish to sell your online business, your accounting records will be carefully scrutinized and can be a deal breaker if they are not detailed and organized. Accurate and organized accounting records are the spine to any business – without them, a business cannot survive.

9

Creating a Marketing Plan

I briefly mentioned this in an earlier chapter, but the most potent form of marketing you can master is word of mouth. Not only is it FREE, but who will consumers listen to more: their best friend telling them how great your product is or an online advertisement? When consumers hear a positive review about a product from someone they know, that review is given more weight than any type of advertisement because their friend or family member does not have (in most cases) any intentions of pushing them to purchase that product for personal benefit.

So how can you take advantage of this powerful form of marketing? It is by selling quality products coupled with professional service – that simple. When customers truly enjoy their experience, they will recommend your online business to their friends who have similar interests. Think about a product you were astonished by in the past, and more likely than not, you told numerous individuals about your delight for that product.

Excluding word of mouth marketing, most online businesses need to have some type of budget to advertise their products. Due to the rapidly changing nature of technology, certain advertisement methods can lose effectiveness with time, so I will discuss more generalized concepts on where and how to market.

The emergence of social media has presented very specialized and targeted marketing opportunities; however, the more targeted your marketing campaign, the more it will cost you. With any type of advertisement, the benefits need to be properly analyzed against the costs to see if it will not only be cost-effective, but also if your money could be better spent elsewhere. A benefit to social media marketing is the ability to attract customers to purchase your products while building a social following at the same time. A strong following on a social media platform can be a great way to consistently reach your target audience that has already expressed interest in your products.

Marketing campaigns can be as vast and creative as you like; however, you need to consider the size of your budget and what type of strategy will be most effective. You should test different "paid" marketing ideas slowly in order to see which provide you the best results without using too much of your allotted funds. While most people think of marketing as something that costs money, there are countless ways to do "free" advertising. One example is by promoting another online business' products that are complimentary to yours in exchange for their promotion of your products. Say your online business specializes in selling iPhone accessories – partnering with another online business that repairs damaged iPhones would be a great cross-promotion opportunity. A customer that pays to fix his iPhone is likely to be interested in iPhone accessories and vice versa. Consumer awareness and sales will increase for both online businesses while spending nothing to gain this advantage – quite the cost-effective form of marketing.

When you create an advertisement, study the attributes of previously successful ads (ideally in your industry but also universally) to understand what made them such a hit. The best advertisements are those that strike a significant human emotion and leave an impactful memory with the viewer. In whatever form possible, if you can associate your advertisement with some type of human emotion, it will see better results.

It takes time to think of creative ideas, so do not rush this process and foolishly waste money. Decide what type of advertisement you want, how long you will run it for, and what message you are trying to get across to your target audience. After running the advertisement, evaluate its results to see if the cost was worth the gained benefits. There is not always a direct correlation between sales and marketing costs, and this especially holds true with certain industries, but you still need some method of evaluation after each ad campaign.

From my own experience, my favorite form of advertising is marketing to customers you have already transacted with. It is mainly cost-free, and it results in a high conversion rate because they are already familiar with your online business. For example, with each item you sell, include a coupon in the shipping package offering customers a discount or free item if they purchase from you again within a specified number of days. Implementing a time constraint will result in a higher percentage of usage because customers will not want this limited opportunity to expire and will thus be more likely to take action. The discount or free item offered does not need to be anything significant, just the fact that it is offered is enough to spark customers to purchase again. With my online business, the coupon I included with each order offered the customer a free gift if they came back and purchased again within 30 days. I saw overwhelmingly better results offering the free gift instead of a 5% or 10% discount, despite the fact that the customer would have saved far more money with the discount. When a customer used the free gift coupon, I included in their package a free Pokémon card that cost in the range of $0.25. Customers loved the excitement of a free gift (and what the free card was too), and I gained not only an extra sale at almost no cost, but more importantly, a loyal customer.

In addition, you will want to email your customers – specifically those who never used the coupon included in their package – on a quarterly basis with a special discount. Offering this occasional discount will help remind these past customers to return to your store and also results in them purchasing more than they normally would in a given order size. It is important to note that you should not overdo the amount of discounts and promotions you offer unless that is your business model. If you do, it can cause your customers to only want to purchase your products when they are offered at a discount, which they know will be frequent, and it can backfire on your sales and profit margins. Promotions on a quarterly basis balance the frequency and predictability of discounts very well, and this time cycle produced the best results for my online business.

Between utilizing word of mouth marketing, advertisement campaigns, and special promotions, you will have a strong marketing strategy enacted to attract both new and repeat customers.

10

Hiring Employees

While you may not need to hire employees for a while, it is valuable for you to see the importance of them, what to look for when hiring, and how they can build or destroy an eventual empire you hope to create.

Employees are costly, not just in terms of money but also in the initial upfront time required to train them. They need adequate instructing, formal procedures in place to follow, and most likely a manager – unless you plan to add that position to your current responsibilities. If you go the route of giving equity ownership to an employee, that is an entirely different situation than the type I will be describing here. Equity ownership correlates to vested interest in the business, thus the individual who has equity ownership needs to have significant responsibilities, and you also have to consider the long-term ramifications from giving up a percentage of your business. While some of these tips regarding employees may apply to the equity ownership situation, this section is predominantly focused on the hiring of either hourly or salaried employees.

I view employees as both a fixed and variable cost – fixed in that you commit hours of time training them and monitoring their work (hopefully only in the beginning), and variable in the obvious sense of the hourly or annual compensation. The value employees provide needs to outweigh the hours you give up to teach and pay them.

Employees are not a necessity in the beginning; however, it depends on your business model and how many people are needed to ensure its success. People often assume the only way to grow is through hiring, which is the unarguable case in the long-run, but in the short-run, you first need to create a proven business record that has scalability and potential before looking to add employees. Once you succeed with that, you will obtain a clearer image of the type of "mundane" work that can be delegated to a new hire.

The two overarching types of employees are those that are specialists (example: IT, marketing, product development, etc.) and those employees that do the more procedural, task-based work (example: shipping items, counting inventory, etc.) The best approach in identifying what part of your online business needs an employee is by accessing the areas of work where you provide the most value, and then assigning the other tasks to someone else. These other tasks should ideally be either the most time consuming for you, least value-adding, or both. For example, if you provide the most value and expertise through your extensive knowledge on how to make or acquire products, then you should focus more of your time on that and delegate the other work the best you can. With my online business, I often acquired thousands of collectible cards at a time, and they all needed to be numerically organized so they could be stored in my inventory system. This was a very time-consuming and tedious process, and when I was in college, I began to hire occasional part-time employees to assist me with this work. This greatly freed up my time and allowed me to focus on all the other parts of my online business where I had very specialized knowledge.

When you begin the process of interviewing applicants, take these interviews very seriously. Entrepreneurs can get so excited by the prospect of having an added employee help their online business grow that they jump at the first resume they see - not realizing it takes sufficient time to find the right person and that employees have the ability to cause more harm than good. It is a necessity you hire an individual who expresses passion for your online business and has a desire to contribute and help it succeed. If the candidate is void of enthusiasm, his/her lack of commitment will be noticeable when difficulties arise. This will also result in high employee turnover, which only forces you to restart the process of interviewing and training, thus wasting even more time. Along with enthusiasm and passion, an important attribute to look for in candidates is their time management skills and ability to learn quickly. If employees can learn the tasks you teach them efficiently while also being able to manage their time well, it will translate into an online business that grows faster on lower costs – a perfect recipe for success.

Even after you have properly trained your employees, it is critical you provide them with continuous feedback. Nothing is more helpful to employees than frequent evaluations about their work – especially in the beginning when they are forming certain habits. Provide them with both positive and constructive feedback, and you will shape the clay of your employees into the end result you desire. Be understanding with difficulties they experience (to an extent) and form a friendly work environment that fosters creativity and openness, but always be strict when necessary. If you allow your employees to "get away with things," they will push boundaries more frequently, and soon enough the culture of your business will change. Employees, even at a large company, can destroy a culture and brand over time. Be cordial yet respected by all those who work for you, and create an example for your employees to follow. If you do, the inevitable issues will be kept to a minimum.

11

The Entrepreneurial Mindset

Being an entrepreneur has been idealized since the technology boom of the late 1990s – society has this glamorized view of the entrepreneurial life. People think having the ability to "set your own schedule" and do as you please means your quality of life is better. Let me briefly state that one's quality of life is dependent on the choices he/she makes. Your habits become your way of life. If you do not wake up with excitement each morning to accomplish the day, you need to reassess your passion. People who are pursuing their passion live a high-quality life and a feeling of fulfillment embodies them.

The life of an entrepreneur is often more demanding than a typical job. You work around the clock and through the weekend – and days off are limited. But with such enjoyment for what you do, does it not make sense that you would want to do all day what brings you the most joy? Remove this mentality that life is easy and money is abundant as an entrepreneur – you need to work as hard as you possibly can and only then will the possibility for success slowly blossom around you.

On the journey to starting your own online business, you will face challenges that have the ability to break you if you are not mentally tough. This journey is not a sprint but a marathon, and the potential successes you foresee will not come as you expect. In the process of building my online business, I could have never foreseen my expansion, opportunities, and life lessons that arose over the years, or the problems that would occur in the process; however, I worked relentlessly on improvement and spent as much time as I could trying to operate a more efficient and value-adding online business.

When you feel the desire to take action, DO IT. You will not have as much energy to follow through on an idea in the future as you will when you initially thought of it, so do what you can to start working on it. The small steps of success achieved throughout the process will increase your confidence to tackle larger challenges, and ever so slowly, that large challenge will be accomplished. Breaking down large tasks into manageable small tasks is the best approach to achievement.

As you work, you will never have all the answers, but you will uncover them along the way – altering and adapting to the changing environment around you. Never settle for the success you experience in the moment as there is always a competitor waiting to steal market share. When a business becomes complacent, it loses its drive to innovate and put in the necessary sweat equity that drove the business to that level of success in the first place.

Lastly, make it a habit to think about your online business throughout the day and ideas will naturally come to you at the most random of times. There were countless incidences throughout the years with my online business where I suddenly thought of a new opportunity while I was sleeping, in class, or walking the streets. With your brain relentlessly focused and absorbed in your business, your mind will subconsciously spark innovative thoughts. Over an extended period of time, you will have an abundance of ideas (some that work and some that do not) that will give your online business the opportunities and change needed to break plateaus and exponentially grow.

12

Conclusion

I would like to congratulate you on having both the desire to run your own online business and for taking productive action by reading this book. Applicable to both business and life, reading is the key ingredient to success. Books provide us with vast knowledge on any subject along with guidance from the trials and tribulations of others. Think of this book as a shortcut to success – I had to spend 12 years of failing and succeeding to accumulate this framework of knowledge, but you had the ability to acquire this information in just a few hours of reading. If you learn from the mistakes of others, you can position yourself to avoid the same missteps in the future.

As you work on growing your online business, understand that all businesses are like puzzles – if you are missing one piece (i.e. customer service, a quality product, fast shipping, etc.), the puzzle will not be complete and your online business will not be operating at its most profitable or efficient level. To be the most successful, you need all components, like all pieces of the puzzle, to be congruent and aligned.

With your newly acquired foundation of knowledge, you are ready to pave your own path to success. Utilize this book as a resource, but recognize that failure will be your best teacher if you choose to listen and reflect on your personal experiences. It is up to you to undertake the process of finding the right type of online business to start given your passion and personal situation. It may not be the first online business you start, but if you keep trying, you will know when you found it.

I wish you the best of luck in your pursuit, and I know you will triumph!

For business inquiries, please contact me at:

Email: mslaughter.business@gmail.com

Made in the USA
Middletown, DE
04 November 2026

36535575R00038